PORTVILLE FREE LIBRARY
PORTVILLE, N. Y.

DISCARDED FROM THE
PORTVILLE FREE LIBRARY

The First Book of New World Explorers

THE FIRST BOOK OF NEW WORLD EXPLORERS

by LOUISE DICKINSON RICH

Pictures by Cary

FRANKLIN WATTS, INC.
845 Third Avenue, New York, N.Y. 10022

Library of Congress Catalog Number: 60–9389

© Copyright 1960 by Louise Dickinson Rich

Printed in the United States of America

SBN 531–00595–X

9 10 11 12 13

Contents

1. Explorers All   1
2. The Vikings   4
3. Before Columbus   12
4. Columbus   20
5. The Spaniards   29
6. Magellan   48
7. The French   54
    Other Books To Read   73
    Acknowledgments   74
    Index   75

The First Book of New World Explorers

1

Explorers All

EVERYBODY is born with a certain amount of the explorer in him. As soon as he can creep, a baby becomes curious about what lies beyond the safe blanket his mother has spread for him on the grass; he goes crawling off to investigate the shadows under the shrubbery. Boys and girls like nothing better than a strange beach or an unknown woodland or, if they live in the city, a different park or a block outside their own neighborhood to explore. There is always the chance that here they will find something new and exciting, something far more wonderful than anything they have ever seen before. We all begin life as explorers.

Most people, as they grow older, lose this instinct. Other things take up their time and attention, and they get out of the habit of wondering what lies around the next corner. They feel that *there* won't be very different from *here,* and that it's hardly worth the bother and risk of going to see. But in every age there have been a few persons who never outgrew the special qualities that make an explorer. Today, with very few unexplored places left on the face of the earth, men and women of this sort seek out those few places, to conquer them. Tenzing Norgay and Sir Edmund Hillary risked their lives to climb Mount Everest not because they had to for any reason that most people would understand, but because an inner feeling drove them.

You might think that when every last inch of the earth has finally been mapped, the breed of explorers would die out for lack of a place to explore; but true explorers will always find something new to investigate. "After all," they think, "the earth isn't so very big. All around it are vast areas of space about which we know little. Let's explore space!" Men are already making preparations to do this.

The early exploration of the Americas and the exploration of space may seem to be two very different matters. Actually they are alike in many ways. The same kind of men will have faced many of the same difficulties and dangers in both cases. All explorers must have certain qualities. They must be brave; they must be curious; they must be intelligent and imaginative; and they must be very tough, both in body and in mind. As to their problems: no matter what place a person explores, he must have some practical means of getting there, whether that means be a ship or a rocket, and he must have a way that he hopes will get him back. He must have food to eat and water to drink and suitable clothing to wear, whether his path leads him into the heat of the equator or the bitter cold between the earth and the moon.

He must have weapons against whatever enemies he meets, whether they be hostile Indians or deadly radiations. He must, in short, have equipment, supplies, and information that he trusts to take him to his destination and to bring him home again.

All an explorer can do is trust. The great danger and the great fascination of exploring is that nobody really *knows* what will be met, so that even the best preparations leave something to chance. The early explorers of the New World may have had to take even more risks than the space explorers of tomorrow will, as we shall see.

2

The Vikings

ALMOST a thousand years ago, in the year 986, a Norse Viking named Bjarni Herjulfson decided to spend the winter with his father, Herjulf, who lived in Iceland—or so Bjarni thought. Bjarni had been away at sea and did not know—since men on voyages had no way of communicating with the folks back home in those days—that his father had moved to Greenland with Eric the Red, a chieftain who had been banished from Iceland for killing a man in a brawl. Greenland was a long way to go, and winter is not the best time to cross the North Atlantic. When he found his father gone, however, Bjarni turned his ship to the west.

This ship was probably the *knorr* type of Viking vessel, built especially for sailing heavy seas. *Knorrs* were high-decked ships, rather broad and tubby, and able to carry a larger sail than the graceful, slender longboats which we usually think of as Viking ships. *Knorrs* ranged from sixty to over a hundred feet in length.

The Vikings sailed the heavy seas in knorrs

Bjarni's ship was probably about ninety feet long. It was tightly built of overlapping oak planks firmly held to sturdy oak ribs by iron rivets. It probably had a large steering oar, controlled by a tiller on the right-hand side of the stern, which was the steerboard. Even today we call the right-hand side of ships the "starboard" side.

Ships in Bjarni's day furnished little shelter for the sailors. The men probably spent most of their time in the open. The provisions were no doubt stored under cured skins and canvaslike pieces of cloth. From the deck rose a single mast for the square, red-and-white-striped sail, which was secured with walrus-hide ropes.

The provisions piled in the middle of the boat probably consisted of tubs of salt pork and corned beef, dried or pickled fish, smoked hams, cheeses, loaves of hard bread, dried fruits and berries, grain and a quern for grinding it, and of course kegs of water and ale. Sometimes in those days a cow was taken along to provide fresh milk or, if the voyage was longer than planned, fresh meat. This meant carrying hay to feed her; so you can see that the boats were rather crowded. It is no wonder that no provision was made for building a fire. It would have been dangerous in such close quarters.

But the Vikings were tough, and eating cold, raw food was no great hardship for them. To keep warm they wore thick woolen clothes and fleece-lined leather jackets, and lined boots on their feet. Their heavy blond beards protected their faces, and operating the ship in the stormy winter seas kept their blood circulating vigorously.

Bjarni's crew was not afraid to start out on an uncharted course in mid-winter. It was the sort of adventure they loved. They had complete confidence in their own seamanship and in their vessel, and rightly so. The Vikings were the best sailors in the world at that time and had the best ships.

One thing Bjarni and his crew could not control, however, was the weather. After leaving Iceland they sailed for three days, then ran into a great fog. Today this would not have made much difference. Now, thanks to radar, radio, and other modern devices, a ship always knows where it is and where it is going, no matter how poor the visibility. But a thousand years ago a mariner did not even have a compass. He depended on the positions of the sun, moon, and stars to guide him. Since Bjarni could not catch a glimpse of these, he had to navigate by guesswork, which is never very dependable.

When at last the fog lifted, he found himself off a low, forest-covered shore. Although he had never been to Greenland, Bjarni was sure that this shore was the wrong place; it did not answer the description he had been given. Because he was in a hurry, he did not land but put out to sea again. Two days later the sailors saw more land. Bjarni did not think that this was Greenland any more than he had the first place. He refused to go ashore, and again the men sailed out to sea. Three days later they saw still more land, this time high and mountainous and with ice on it. Still Bjarni would not land. Finally, after several more days, the voyagers reached a place that looked to Bjarni as if it might be Greenland. That evening, according to ancient Norse tales, he came to a shore under a cape which had a boat on it, and there on the cape lived Bjarni's father.

Apparently, when Bjarni told people where he and his men had been and what they had seen, nobody was much interested.

In their rovings the Vikings often saw unfamiliar coasts. Nevertheless, the land that Bjarni Herjulfson sighted was without doubt North America—probably a part of New England, Nova Scotia, and Newfoundland. He and his crew were the first Europeans ever to reach the mainland of that continent.

It was not until fifteen years later, in the year 1000, that Eric the Red's son Leif, who had meanwhile grown up, heard about Bjarni's voyage and wondered about it. He thought that Bjarni had been lacking in curiosity not to land and explore the shore. Leif bought a ship from Bjarni Herjulfson. He collected a crew of thirty-five men and set sail. In time he came to a coast of flat ledges, which he called Helluland, or Land of Bare Rocks, and which was probably Labrador. But since Bjarni had mentioned forests, Leif turned southward and soon came to a densely wooded shore. Trees were scarce in both Greenland and Iceland, and Leif was so impressed by them that he named the place Markland, or Woodland, although we know it as Nova Scotia.

Leif was a true explorer, and he was not content merely to prove that the land he had heard of really existed. He wanted to know more about it. He continued south along the coast, plowing through the rough seas that pounded in thunderous surf against the crags of the unknown shore. Finally he arrived at a place so promising that he decided to build huts and spend the winter. There was wonderful fishing and hunting; the weather seemed very mild compared to Greenland; and the woods were full of more wild grapes than any of the crew had ever seen. They named the place Vinland, or Wineland. It was probably part of the coast of New England, but no one is sure exactly what part. Because of the abundance of grapes and because the Vikings made special mention later of the long hours of daylight during the winter, most authorities believe it to have been Massachusetts, where the winter days are noticeably longer than in Greenland. Wherever it was, the visitors seem to have spent a comfortable and pleasant time. Other Viking voyagers apparently followed them later, found Leif's huts, and stayed in them for longer or shorter periods.

That being the case, why didn't they establish permanent colonies in this land that was so much more fertile and so much easier to live in than Greenland or Iceland? The reason was partly that the Vikings were rovers and fighters, not colonists. They had left Norway for Iceland in the first place only because King Harald Fairhair had gained control of the country and had started to rule it with a ruthless hand. Later Eric the Red had moved on to Greenland not because he wanted to, but because he had to, on account of his killing. Vinland lay at the end of a long and difficult voyage and there seemed no reason to start a permanent colony there.

The Greenlanders did lack timber for building ships and houses, however, and they could get this from the New World. For several centuries trips were made to North America, and lumber was brought back. In the course of their journeys the

Vikings made further explorations and they may even have had several small colonies. No one is quite sure of this.

In the end, however, their voyages stopped. The native Algonquin Indians became more and more resentful of the intruders, and began to attack landing parties. Fierce fighters though they were, the Vikings were outnumbered; they had no better weapons than the Indians and they were on unfamiliar ground. They lost skirmishes that later explorers with the advantage of firearms might have won. At about the same time, famine set in at home and the native Eskimos of Greenland, with whom the Vikings had been on bad terms for four hundred years, raised a huge army and completely wiped out the Norse settlements, driving the Vikings back to Iceland and Norway. These places were too far from North America to make ocean trips worth while; the trips ceased altogether, and in the next few centuries the New World was all but forgotten.

The Indians attacked landing parties

3

Before Columbus

AFTER the Vikings stopped going to Markland and Vinland, a long time passed before other Europeans ventured into the Western Hemisphere. The chief reason for this was an almost total ignorance of what the world was really like. It is not true that everybody believed it to be flat, spinning through space like a flying saucer. There were people who recognized that the earth was a globe, but their knowledge was a theory that had never been put to a practical test and was unheard of by a majority of the common people. In our own day, scientists working in laboratories knew about nuclear fission long before ordinary folks dreamed of such a thing; and so it was then. The information about the earth's true shape had not filtered down to everyday levels; and even if it had, the arguments in proof of it were difficult for uneducated people to understand.

The popular notion of the earth was something like this. It was a large disk, with Europe and Asia in the center. All around the edges of the disk were either vast deserts, thick swamps, or the ocean, which was called *Mare Tenebrosum,* or the Sea of Darkness. This name did not mean that the ocean was really dark like the night, but that it was mysterious and threatening. Sailors had noticed that as they went north the temperature became colder, and as they went south it became increasingly hot. So they guessed that if they sailed far enough north they would come to a high mountain of ice; and if they continued far enough south they would come to a sea of flame and boiling water. If they went too far east or west, naturally they would fall off the edge of the disk.

The maps of the time did nothing to encourage the timid. In more recent centuries, map makers simply leave unknown areas

blank, with the words "Unexplored Territory" printed across them. But the early map makers, when they had no facts, used their imaginations. Around the unexplored fringes of their maps they drew dragons and horrible monsters. There were unipeds—manlike creatures with one leg ending in a foot like an umbrella, on which they took gigantic hops; and Cyclopes with a single blazing eye in their foreheads; and men with no heads at all who carried their eyes and mouths in their stomachs; and ravenous harpies with the heads of women and the bodies of birds. Then there was the deadly upas tree, which was supposed to rain death on any person so foolish as to seek its inviting shade. Sometimes the map artist simply wrote "Unicorns here," words frightening enough to scare any sailor; and sometimes in a stretch of open ocean the artist would warn "Loadstone mountain." A loadstone is magnetic, and people supposed that here were whole mountains of loadstone—powerful magnets which pulled the nails out of a ship so that it fell to pieces and sank. All these labels may seem silly to us, but the sailors of that time believed what they read on a map. It is not surprising that they felt safer in familiar waters.

Actually there were plenty of real dangers to worry about without imagining more. To the west was the Sargasso Sea, a tremendous area of floating seaweed. Here sailors supposed that ships could be caught for days or weeks while their food supplies slowly dwindled. There really were not giant fish with huge suckers in their heads hiding beneath the seaweed and holding the vessels fast, or enormous squid waiting to encircle them with their long arms. But the sailors believed in these things, and this terror was added to the threat of starvation if the ships were held in the seaweed.

Ships did fall to pieces and sink at sea, not because of loadstones, but because of the teredos, or shipworms. These pierced and ate through the toughest oak planking until a vessel that looked sound might really be nothing but a shell. Today's metal-sheathed boats are proof against shipworms; they did not bother the Vikings either, since shipworms are not common in icy northern seas.

Neither were the Vikings troubled much with scurvy, a disease, caused by lack of vitamins, which sometimes killed half the crew of a southern European ship. In the narrower North Atlantic, unbroken voyages were seldom longer than two weeks or so, as the islands—the Shetlands, the Faroes, Iceland, and Greenland—served as supply bases where fresh food could be obtained. There also the cool climate preserved meats and vegetables for fairly long periods. Further south there were few places where a ship on a long voyage could take on new provisions, and foods spoiled rapidly in the heat. Sailors lived almost entirely on heavily salted meat and hard biscuits that soon became wormy. On lengthy journeys the drinking water in the wooden tanks became green, foul, and slimy. Even when the poor diet did not cause scurvy, it undermined the health of the men so badly that a small cut or rope burn often resulted in blood poisoning or gangrene. A few long voyages could ruin a sailor's health for the rest of his life.

The ships of the fifteenth century were rather chunky in shape, and in rough weather they pitched and rolled so badly that seasoned sailors were often seasick. To add to their discomfort, the men were crowded into damp, evil-smelling quarters overrun with rats and crawling with lice. Cotton was rare and expensive, and a sailor's clothing was of wool, which caused bad cases of prickly heat and the itch and which attracted lice. A man could wash his clothes, but only in salt water, which made the garments sticky and stiff so that they irritated his skin further.

The continuous discomfort, in addition to inhumanly long and irregular hours, cruelly hard work, constant wettings, and dreadful monotony with nothing to read and nothing to do brought on what was known as "sailors' vapors," a highly nervous condition that led to frequent fights. To keep any sort of order, a captain had to use harsh methods of punishment. All in all, sailors had miserable lives, and it is no wonder that they were unenthusiastic about long trips into unexplored regions.

The ships' officers had their troubles, too. They were expected to bring their vessels safely home from voyages, navigating under the handicaps of unreliable charts, unwieldy sailing ships, tough and surly crews, and almost no instruments. They did have magnetic compasses, and very crude quadrants called cross-staffs were in use too, for calculating latitude. These latter were inaccurate when the ship rolled, however, and since the ship rolled a good

The sailors led miserable lives

deal of the time it was easy for a captain to get far off course without realizing it.

Longitude was even harder to determine, as there were no chronometers to mark differences in time. Instead, a ship's boy was assigned the task of turning a sandglass every half hour, the very second the last grain of sand ran through from its upper section to its lower. As this was a boring job and boys are apt to be careless anyhow, they often forgot all about the glass until too late, and so the keeping of time was not accurate. Ship logs for measuring speed were unknown. To figure the speed of a boat, a man tossed a chip of wood overboard from the bow and counted the number of his own heartbeats until the chip came abreast of the stern. Or he watched a clump of seaweed or some other object in the water, and tried to estimate his speed by that.

Hampered by these lacks, a master mariner of those days had to depend largely on dead reckoning, and it was the practice to sail due north or south to the parallel on which the ship's destination lay, then turn at right angles and follow the parallel straight east or west. One error in calculation could throw a ship badly off course, and once it was lost or in difficulty there was no way for it to summon aid from other ships in the vicinity. Each vessel was entirely on its own.

All these things—the real and imagined perils, the small, uncomfortable ships, the true hardships of long voyages, the lack of knowledge of the earth and navigation—held men back from sailing west. Besides, there was no urgent need to do so.

People lived comfortably enough in the world as they knew it, and had nothing much to gain by foolhardy ventures. But in 1453 the Ottoman Turks captured Constantinople and were free to cut off the old overland trade routes to the Orient. What trade still existed was in the hands of the Italian cities. This changed the whole face of things.

Now most of the countries of Europe were prevented from trading in the luxuries that came only from Asia: silks, jewels, pearls, rich rugs, and dyes. Even more important were the spices of the East, now no longer easy to obtain. In our day of canned or frozen foods and good refrigeration we do not depend on spices as the ancients did. Then food had little variety, cooking methods were primitive and unskilled, and lack of cooling systems allowed meat to spoil rapidly. Rich and poor alike disguised the flavor of their food by generous use of nutmeg, ginger, clove, mace, cinnamon, allspice, and especially pepper. Without these spices it was almost impossible to cook a meal fit for even the least particular person to eat. Spices were a necessity.

As there seemed to be no hope of overthrowing the Turks or of getting the spice trade away from the Italian merchants, only one course remained for the other European countries. They must find a new way to reach the Orient. Although it sounded insane to most people, there were those who believed that the best way to reach the East would be to sail west.

4

Columbus

ONE of the believers in a westward route was Christopher Columbus, the son of an Italian weaver. Rightfully, Christopher should have become a weaver, too; but he found the harbor and wharves of his native city of Genoa much more interesting than his father's looms. He spent long hours around the waterfront, learning about ships and the making of maps and charts, which were in great demand. Occasionally he shipped before the mast on a short voyage here or there. His interest in seafaring and map-making led him, when he was a young man, to settle in Portugal as a chartmaker and mariner.

The world of those days was humming with new ideas, and Columbus may well have heard talk of lands to the west. In any case, he became convinced that the earth was a globe. This belief might have come to nothing, however, if he had not married the daughter of the Captain of the tiny island of Porto Santo and gone to live there, three hundred miles out in the Atlantic Ocean. For the son of a poor Italian weaver to marry the daughter of a Portuguese nobleman was almost unheard of in those days, but Columbus was very charming and strikingly handsome. He was tall and broad-shouldered, with lively blue-gray eyes, high color, and by the time he was thirty, snow-white, curly hair. Any girl would have been impressed with him.

What is important to us, however, is the way that living on Porto Santo affected Columbus. There, washed up on the beaches from who knew where, he saw strangely carved blocks of wood, and plants and trees not native to his part of the world. And he was told of the bodies of two persons, also found on the shore. They looked utterly unlike any Europeans or any known African tribes. Here were things a person could see and touch, far more convincing to him than rumors or the theories of the geographers that there really was a land beyond the Sea of Darkness. His imagination was fired, and he was seized with a fever to find the East Indies by sailing west.

This ambition ruled the next years of his life. He could not rest until he had found a way to carry it out. The voyage he had in mind would cost a great deal of money, much more than Columbus had. He must find someone to pay his expenses. The best people to approach, he thought, would be the rulers of various countries. These people were rich, and they ought to be interested in controlling the spice trade for their nations. When he suggested his idea, however, no one showed great enthusiasm, and

Strange things were washed up on Porto Santo's beaches

it was not until he was almost penniless and nearly discouraged that he won the support of Queen Isabella of Spain.

Still no one was eager to risk his ship in this venture. The Queen solved this problem by deciding to punish the seaport of Palos for several things its people had done to displease her. She demanded that they provide two furnished ships for the undertaking.

The *Niña* and the *Pinta,* of Palos, were impressed into the service of the Crown, and Columbus chartered a third ship, the *Santa Maria.* Then came the business of finding crews. The names of those who sailed with Columbus are known today from records; most of them seem to have been men and boys from Palos and its neighboring ports—tough and ready folk, reared beside the sea and trained from childhood as seamen; men with a sense of adventure and a hope of bettering themselves by this voyage.

In August, 1492, the three ships set sail. The ninety-foot *Santa Maria,* which was the largest, served as Columbus' flagship. Next in size was the *Pinta;* and smallest was the *Niña,* or "Baby." The vessels journeyed straight south for a way, then turned west to their destination, Cipangu, or Japan. Columbus assured the men that it would not be a long voyage. Oddly enough, all the geographers had made the same error in calculating the size of the globe and had arrived at an answer almost one-fourth too small. Columbus thought he was telling the truth.

A few days from port the *Pinta* reported that her rudder had broken, and the little fleet put in to the Canary Islands to make repairs. The *Pinta's* rudder was mended and a new sail rig was put on the *Niña,* to make her easier to handle in the wind. More wood, food, and water were put aboard the ships, and they were ready to put out into the Atlantic.

Few of the sailors had been this far from the mainland before, and Columbus knew that a day would come when their voyage into the unknown would make them uneasy and difficult to manage. He therefore kept two sets of figures for the number of miles traveled each day—one for himself, and a much smaller one that he let the sailors see so that they would not know how far from home they really were.

At first the voyage went well, and the ships made good time. But when they came to the Sargasso Sea, the men began to grumble. Here the ocean was one great mass of tough green and yellow seaweed, and they feared that the ships might become stuck and never be able to get out. Many small crabs lived in the seaweed. Columbus caught some of them and nailed them to the mast where everyone could see them. Crabs, he said, lived mostly on land, so the shore must be very near. These dead crabs would be reminders of the fact.

Next the ships ran out of the trade winds and entered an area of calms and variable winds. The little fleet made poor time here, but Columbus looked on the bright side of the situation. Previously, when the ships had been bowling along blown by the trade winds, the men had begun to be afraid they would never be able to sail back to Spain against these gales. Now here was proof that the winds did not always blow hard in one direction. But the men grumbled more and more. Some whispered that it would be a good thing if Columbus fell overboard some dark night.

The men grumbled to each other

It must have been a dreadfully lonely time for him. He was a single Italian in a group of hostile Spaniards who spared his life only because they doubted whether they could ever find their way home without him. The voyage could have been a pleasure if only his companions had been as confident and eager as he himself was. Then they would have welcomed the varying fortunes of the trip westward. The foul water, wormy hardtack, and cramped quarters would have seemed merely annoyances in a splendid adventure. As it was, Columbus had to scheme and plot all by himself, wondering every minute how much longer he could keep control of the situation. The ten weeks of the voyage must have seemed almost endless to him.

On October 10 a committee faced Columbus and told him that if he did not turn back they would have to take matters into their own hands. With difficulty he persuaded them to go just a little way further. And then, as he wrote in his log book, "God stretched out his arm." On October 11 a flight of small land birds skimmed past, and a little later a fresh-cut pole and a small carved board were picked up, and the men saw a green reed and a

A flight of land birds skimmed by

berry-covered branch. Even the most stupid person knew that these were signs of nearby land. And when Columbus promised a silk doublet in addition to the cash prize that the King and Queen had offered to the first man who sighted land, everyone forgot about a mutiny in straining his eyes to win the reward.

At about two hours before midnight on October 11 Columbus thought he saw a light, but it seemed so flickering and uncertain that he could not be sure. A few hours later, at two o'clock on the morning of October 12, 1492, an ordinary seaman named Juan Rodriguez Bermejo raised a shout. About six miles ahead he could see in the brilliant moonlight a glimmer of sandy beach and breaking surf. A gun spoke from the vessel in celebration, and the ships all shortened sail and dropped anchor to wait for the dawn to break over what they believed would be Japan but what was really a whole new and undreamed-of world.

Columbus himself never set foot on North America. What he thought was Japan was one of what we now call the Bahamas. He was never to know the true extent of his discovery. Political scheming and the death of his friend Isabella finally robbed him of further aid from the Crown. In 1506, after three more voyages, he died, his health broken by hardship and his heart broken by the treachery and unfulfilled promises of those he had trusted.

But no one can rob him of the honor and credit of discovering the New World. He did not stumble on it accidentally as the Vikings had done. He had set out deliberately to find what lay over the western horizon. In the face of most people's disbelief

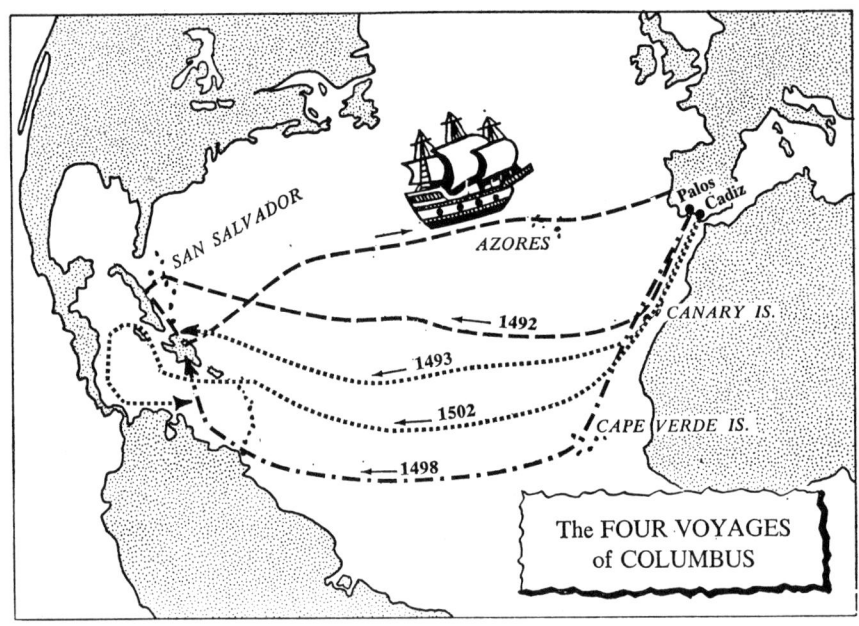

The FOUR VOYAGES of COLUMBUS

and in spite of tremendous obstacles he succeeded. Many brave men followed him later to explore the shores he found for them, but none equaled Columbus in courage, imagination, and perseverance. He went where no European had been before. He was the first, and in daring to be the first he was the greatest.

5

The Spaniards

"EVERYONE who heard of this enterprise said it was a mockery," Columbus wrote rather bitterly after his first voyage. "Now even tailors wish to discover." And it was true that once the way had been shown, many persons and nations decided to investigate what they thought was a new route to Asia.

A few stand out among the many who went. One was John Cabot, an Italian navigator sailing under the English flag. In 1497 he visited the coasts the Vikings knew. His voyage was not important for what he rediscovered, since it would have been visited by someone else sooner or later, but it was important because it gave England a future claim in the New World.

Another navigator was Amerigo Vespucci, an Italian navigator and chartmaker in the employ of Spain. He called the lands he found *Mundus Novus,* or New World, because, he wrote, "among our ancestors there was no knowledge of them." This was the first time the term "New World" had been applied to the Americas; but we remember Amerigo Vespucci best because in 1507 a famous German map maker named the New World "America" for him. Many people used the German maps, and the name America became permanent.

A third explorer was Pedro Alvares Cabral, a Portuguese navigator on whose discoveries in Brazil the later claims of Portugal were based. Still another was Giovanni da Verrazano, an Italian employed by France, who in 1524 explored the coast of North America from the Carolinas to Nova Scotia.

Just as today governments bear the expense of exploratory trips under the Arctic icecap by nuclear-powered submarines or into space by rockets, so in those days governments financed expeditions to the unknown lands across the sea. Each country was anxious to outdistance the rest—as each is today—and a good mariner or trained navigator had no trouble finding work. That is why men so often sailed for countries other than their own. Exploring was a business with them, not a matter of patriotism, and they went about it in a businesslike way, selling their services to the highest bidder.

Spain, largely because she wanted to protect the toe hold she had gained in 1492, was the most active nation in the first fifty years after Columbus' discoveries. It is unwise to say flatly that men of any country all possess the same national traits. The Spanish explorers, however, were of a definite kind. They were cruel and treacherous, yet they were deeply religious. They were almost insanely greedy for gold, yet they would shoe their horses with it or give away a fortune to a friend. They were obstinate and faithless; yet their courage and endurance were almost unbelievable at times. We call them *conquistadors;* they were conquerors as well as explorers, fired with greed. They aimed to wring as much wealth as possible from the New World, and they were not squeamish about the methods they used.

One of these Spaniards was Juan Ponce de León, a veteran of Columbus' second voyage, who came back to colonize Puerto Rico. There he heard an Indian story about a fountain that would make old men young if they simply drank its water. He went looking for this wonderful thing, and on Easter Sunday of 1513 he came within sight of a strange coast. Since Easter is called *Pascua Florida* in Spanish, he named the land Florida. Instead of finding the Fountain of Youth he was mortally wounded by an Indian arrow on a second trip to his newly discovered land, but he left the name Florida forever on the map.

At about the same time, a stowaway was found in a barrel aboard a Spanish ship bound for a colony in South America. He was a tall, red-headed young man named Vasco Nuñez de Balboa, who was fleeing Santo Domingo to avoid being put in jail for his debts. The leader considered marooning him on a desert island, the usual punishment for stowaways, but Balboa seemed so competent that he decided instead to use him. Later he followed Balboa's suggestion that the colony be moved to Panama.

Balboa proved to be a skilled swordsman and a natural-born leader, truly concerned—unlike some Spaniards—with the wel-

Ponce de Leon named the land Florida

fare of his men. One of them said of him, "If a man became worn out or ill, he would not desert him, but looked after him as if he had been a son or a brother." He treated the Indians more mildly than most Spaniards did, too, and won their friendship. They told him of a country to the southwest of Panama where there was so much gold that people used it for drinking cups.

This land could be reached by way of an ocean across the Isthmus of Panama. Naturally, since gold was a passion with the Spanish, Balboa determined to find it.

He set out to cross the isthmus with 190 men, six hundred Indian warriors, a pack of bloodhounds, and his big dog Leoncico. It was terrible country, mountainous and covered with jungle, but the men hacked their way through with their swords, fighting off insects, snakes, and fever. At last, while the exhausted men were resting, Balboa climbed a ridge and saw spread out below him a vast expanse of water. He did not realize that he had discovered the greatest ocean on earth. He called it simply *El Mar del Sur,* the South Sea, and knelt with his men to give thanks to God. Four days later they reached the ocean, and Balboa stepped into its water, claiming "these seas and lands" for Spain.

His discovery delighted the King, but it also aroused the envy of other Spanish adventurers, who set about plotting Balboa's downfall. They were successful. Three years later he was beheaded for treason.

Another of the Spanish conquistadors excited by Indian tales of treasure was Hernán Cortés. He was a handsome young nobleman who in 1519 set out from Cuba with an expedition to subdue the Aztec land of Mexico. On the surface Cortés seemed modest, honest, and religious; but underneath he was arrogant, cruel, and grasping. There is no denying, though, that he was both brave and intelligent.

He was also fortunate. For centuries the Aztecs of Mexico

Balboa's men hacked their way through jungle

had kept alive a legend that a lost god, Quetzalcoatl, would return to them from the eastern sea with a throng of white companions. When Cortés and his men arrived on the Mexican coast in 1519, the Indians believed that the prophecy had come true and they looked upon the invaders with awe and fear, considering them to be immortal. Because the Aztecs had this feeling, Cortés found it much easier to impress them than he might have otherwise.

Working up the coast, Cortés finally established a base on the shore at the village of Vera Cruz, and destroyed all his ships so that his men could not go backward. Now, he told them, they must go forward to Tenochtitlán, which today is Mexico City. Here the Aztec leader, Montezuma, lived and here the Aztec treasure was stored. The long march into the mountains began. There were 450 mail-clad men, six small cannon, and horses and dogs, besides a long train of natives whom Cortés had enslaved to carry his baggage. All this array—the gleaming, arrowproof armor, the white faces, the plumed helmets, and the noisy guns—awed the simple Aztecs; but it was the horses and the dogs that really struck terror to their hearts. The Indians had never seen horses before, and the huge animals with their iron-shod hoofs, rolling white eyes, and tossing manes threw them into a panic. Moreover, though they had small curs of their own, these were nothing like the powerful, well-trained, and vicious Spanish bloodhounds, who could and did kill a man easily. In fact, Cortés' dogs played such a large part in the conquest of Mexico that, when the spoils were divided, each received a crossbowman's share of slaves and gold.

Cortés' party took over two months to reach their goal, and then it was the Spaniards' turn to be amazed. They had not expected to see anything like Tenochtitlán, built on islands in a lake and connected to the mainland by three long causeways. One of the Spaniards later wrote, "It appeared like the enchanted castles which they tell of in books." The houses were of red stone trimmed with white stucco, and because on the island there was little room to spare, the brilliant flower gardens were planted on the flat roofs. Floating vegetable gardens—great rafts covered with rich loam—ringed the island and bore crops of beans, corn, and tomatoes. It was a lovely sight to the jungle-weary eyes of the Spanish.

They crossed the causeway and were welcomed as gods by Montezuma, a tall man of about forty with a light skin, slim body, and pleasant, humorous face. He was richly dressed and hung with ornaments of pure gold and precious jewels. He lodged the Spaniards in a magnificent palace and served them a banquet at which thirty different courses were kept hot in special earthen dishes, much like our double-boilers. Then, like a good host, he showed them over the city, ending at the great pyramid where the gods sat—huge idols of solid gold and silver with jeweled eyes and ornaments.

This sight stirred the Spaniards with a desire to seize the enormous treasure for their own. Soon after, using as an excuse

Montezuma showed the Spanish his city

the fact that the Aztecs made human sacrifices to their gods, Cortés arrested Montezuma and shut him in his palace. The Aztecs became unfriendly, and when Cortés was forced to return to the coast his remaining men became involved in a fight with the Indians. Cortés returned to find the men besieged. When

Montezuma tried to quiet his people, he was stoned and killed.

On a dark night which became known as *la Noche Triste,* or the Sorrowful Night, the Spaniards, carrying much of the city's gold, fought their way across the causeways. Half of them were slaughtered and many more were drowned as they tried to reach the mainland with the sacks of gold they could not bear to leave behind.

A year later, Cortés went back and finally subdued the Aztec stronghold, securing it for Spain. Gold poured into the royal treasury, and the Spanish children had a new toy to play with: Aztec balls—made of "the milk of certain trees"—which would bounce high in the air. This is the first mention made of rubber, which turned out to be far more valuable to the world than all the Aztecs' gold.

But Cortés, who had won an empire by treachery, fell victim to treachery. His enemies poisoned the King's mind against him and he died in poverty and disgrace, leaving his plan to extend Spain's holding to the south to be carried out by another man, Francisco Pizarro.

Pizarro was an uneducated farm boy who had run away from home and arrived in the Indies with no possessions except his cloak and sword. He was a true adventurer, however, bold, ruthless, and clever, and he quickly improved his lot. When rumors were heard of a treasure much greater than that of the Aztecs, Pizarro decided to lead an expedition down the west coast of South America to find it.

His first expedition was a failure, but Pizarro would not give up. He found new partners who backed him for a second journey. After months of hardship, the expedition arrived at Tumbes on the Gulf of Guayaquil. An Inca, one of the ruling class, came to meet them and escorted them through a town as fine as any in Spain. Metal workers were sitting in booths making objects of gold and silver, which these people valued as we do tin or aluminum, because it was useful and not because it would buy other things. Naturally, all this precious metal interested the Spaniards, and when they saw the Temple of the Sun they nearly went mad with greed. It was entirely plated with gold, and all around it was an artificial garden with trees and shrubs fashioned of gold and silver, and with fruit and flowers of precious gems. It must have been beautiful. But Pizarro's force was too small to seize it, and he decided to return to Spain and tell the King of his discoveries.

Three years later he was back, accompanied by his brothers and a band of almost two hundred men. The same old Spanish story of cruelty, treachery, and greed began again. Pizarro's conquest of Peru was made easier by the Incas' wonderful system of roads, better than those of Europe at that time. They ran the entire length of the country, with branches to the sea. Every few miles there were stations where couriers were permanently posted so that messages and goods could be relayed by fast runners in a very short time. In fact, fresh fish was delivered from the sea to cities high in the mountains in less time than it takes

Pizarro's men were astonished at the wealth of the town

to get there by train today; and a message could reach Quito from Cuzco, two thousand miles away, in four days—almost as fast as today's mail. The Spaniards took over these roads for the movement of their own troops and plunder.

Pizarro had learned from Cortés how valuable a good hostage could be. He quickly made an excuse to seize the chief Inca, as Cortés had seized Montezuma. It was a poor excuse, and unfair, too. Pizarro had his friar read a long paper in Spanish, which the Indians could not understand, demanding their conversion to Christianity. Then the friar handed the Inca a Bible. He turned the pages in bewilderment, and not understanding, tossed it to the ground.

The religious Spaniards were horrified. Before the sun set, hundreds of Indians were dead and the Inca, Atahualpa, was a prisoner.

Atahualpa was quick to see that his captors were gold-crazy. He told Pizarro that in return for his freedom he would fill with gold the room in which they sat, as high as he could reach standing on tiptoe. It was a good-sized room, but when Pizarro agreed, long lines of men began coming in from all over Peru, bearing gold on their backs or driving llamas laden with gold. Slowly but surely the room filled with gold dishes and bracelets, statues and ornaments, and even gold nails pulled from the woodwork of the temples.

Now Pizarro was in a quandary. He did not dare free the Inca to lead the Indians against the Spaniards, yet breaking his word

The Spanish seized Atahualpa as a prisoner

was dangerous, too. Finally he decided to put Atahualpa on trial for a list of ridiculous crimes such as hoarding gold that belonged to the King of Spain and having more than one wife. Of course the Inca was found guilty, and was strangled with a bowstring.

From then on Pizarro and his brothers brought the land of the Incas under Spanish control by bloody and treacherous means. They gained great wealth for Spain, but they themselves profited nothing in the end. All except one died by violence: one beheaded, one slain in battle, and Pizarro himself murdered by the daggers of jealous assassins.

It seemed reasonable to the Spaniards that there must be gold to the north of Mexico as well as to the south. This idea was encouraged by Indian stories of seven fabulous cities in what is now the United States Southwest. The Indians delighted in telling tales like this, chiefly in the hope of ridding themselves of their conquerors.

The first to seek the cities was Hernando de Soto, an experienced explorer who had been in Peru with Pizarro. He conducted his search by land from Florida. With about six hundred men, 250 horses, and a pack of bloodhounds he worked his way north through the Carolinas and then west through what are now Tennessee, Alabama, and Mississippi. The Muskogee Indians whom he encountered were not like the civilized Incas and Aztecs. They were savage and warlike, and they lost no time in rallying to defend their homeland. Almost at once de Soto lost nearly one hundred men, and a year later when the Chickasaws attacked him he suffered further great losses.

Finally, in 1542, with over half his men dead, nearly all his equipment lost, and only forty lame and bony horses left, he arrived at a "great river almost half a league wide, deep, rapid, constantly rolling down trees and driftwood on its turbid current." It was the Mississippi. But though he and his men wandered about for some months, the only cities he could find were miserable Indian villages of no wealth at all.

Finally, exhausted and disappointed, de Soto fell ill and died of a fever. So that the Indians would not suspect his death, his men wrapped his body in skins, weighted it with sand, and sank it at midnight in the great river he had discovered. With it sank

De Soto was buried in the river at midnight

the hopes of the expedition. The men floated on rafts down the river to the sea and followed the coastline to Mexico.

Meanwhile another expedition under Francisco Coronado was seeking the same seven cities from a different direction. With three hundred men and the terrible horses, he marched up from Mexico as far as Kansas and Nebraska. Coronado took excellent care of his men, organizing buffalo-hunting parties and finding Indian corn for them. He discovered the Grand Canyon, which he considered a marvelous sight, but a barrier in his path; and he found the seven big pueblos of the Zuñi Indians, which he was forced to conclude must be the famous seven cities. Disgusted by the lack of gold in them, he kept on into the Great

Coronado's men discovered the Grand Canyon

Plains, where the Indian villages of thatched wigwams resembled fabulous cities even less. He thoroughly explored a great deal of beautiful country, but he found no wealth of any sort. Finally he gave up and made his way back to Mexico.

Actually, in contrast to the other conquistadors, he gave more to the land he explored than he took from it. The herds of wild

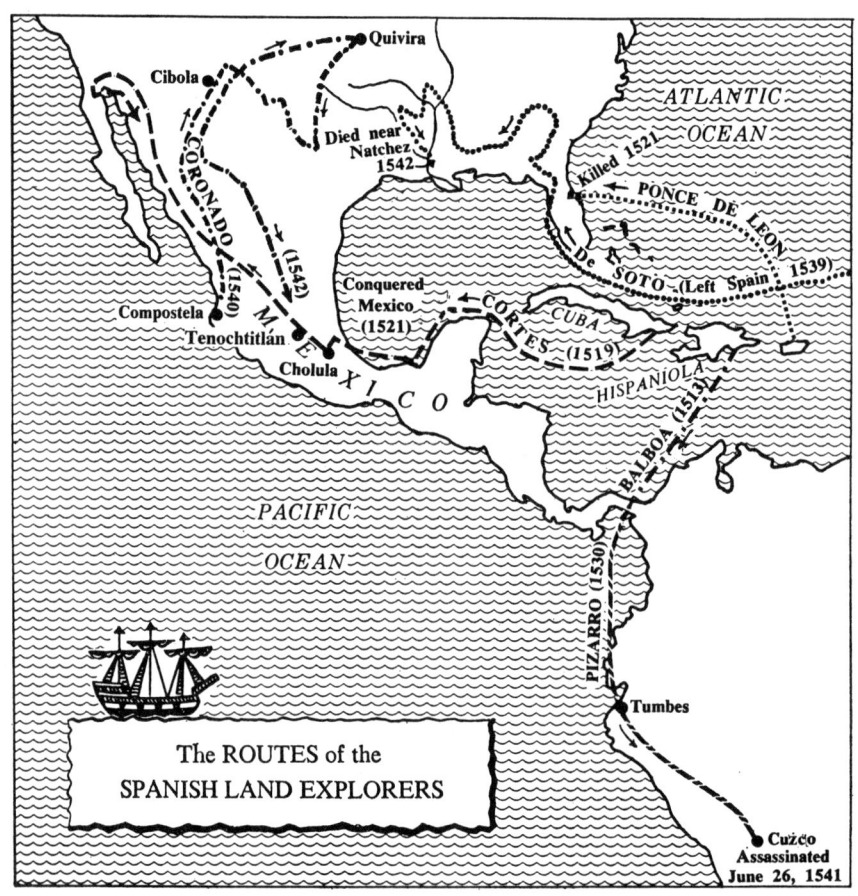

horses which the Indians later tamed were descended from horses that escaped or were turned loose by Coronado. The later use of these mounts entirely changed the Indians' methods of fighting and so had enormous influence on the history and settlement of the West. And unlike most of the other Spaniards, who invited violent ends, Coronado died peacefully in old age.

By the middle of the sixteenth century Spain had a good start toward owning all the Western Hemisphere. Why then did she fail, and her holdings shrink to almost nothing? Partly because of Spanish cruelty and greed. Natives everywhere finally revolted against their conquerors' brutality and bloodshed. Then, too, other countries of Europe were gaining in power and gradually, in a series of wars, Spain lost her position of strength. Traces of Spain remain in the art and speech and faces of some of the people and in some of the names on the map of the Americas; but Spain was not proud master of the New World for very long.

6

Magellan

DURING the years of discovery, people had gradually come to realize that the lands beyond the sea were not a part of Asia but were truly a New World. For a long time, however, they were not interested in the New World for itself. To be sure, they were eager to find what wealth they could there, but at the same time many of them thought of the New World as something of a nuisance—a barrier to any westward route to the East. They did not realize the New World's true size or importance. They chiefly sought a passage through or around its lands so that they might sail to the Spice Islands.

We can look at an accurate modern map and think, "How stupid not to realize the size of the Americas!" But the explorers had no accurate map, and all they could judge by was what they could see: a length of beach backed by a forest, or the loom of a headland. They could not even be sure whether what they were looking at was an island or a cape, let alone a continent.

Columbus showed the way to the New World, but it took many men a long time really to discover the truth about it. What Columbus began was not finished until thirty years later, when Magellan made his tremendous voyage.

Ferdinand Magellan was a Portuguese soldier who served his own country for many years in India, Malay, and Morocco. In Morocco he was lamed for life by a spear wound in the knee. For this or some other reason King Manuel of Portugal refused him further advancement at just the time when Magellan heard about Balboa's discovery and began to suspect that the world was much larger than Columbus had supposed. There might be, he thought, a real ocean between the New World and the Spice Islands near India where he had been stationed. Perhaps if one followed the east coast of South America far enough, one could sail around into Balboa's sea and cross it to the islands.

When King Manuel refused to help Magellan, he took his idea to King Charles V of Spain. Charles assigned him five small ships and 243 men of all nations, including an Italian gentleman named Antonio Pigafetta, who went on the journey for the adventure. Luckily he kept a journal that is a record of the voyage. He tells us that the ships King Charles gave Magellan were old and unseaworthy, and that many of the crew were ruffians, bound to make trouble. They started talking mutiny even before they reached Brazil, and Magellan was obliged to clap one of the captains into irons.

For four months the little fleet sailed down the coast of South

America, entering every large river mouth in the hope that it was a passage to the South Sea, but turning back when the water lost its saltiness. The trip was a discouraging business, and the men's hearts were not in it. They did some exploring of the land, and finally went ashore to winter in a rugged, snowy place. In April, 1520, another mutiny started, and Magellan was forced to kill two of his captains and abandon several guilty leaders ashore. Then he sailed on through violent storms and mountainous seas. One of his ships was wrecked, but Magellan would not give up.

Finally, on October 21, 1520, the explorers found the narrow passage now called the Strait of Magellan. It wound between steep crags and barren plains, and every foot of the way was made dangerous by baffling winds and treacherous currents. But the water remained salt, and Magellan knew he had found what he was seeking. For over a month he struggled to get through the strait's perilous 350 miles. The pilot of one of his ships gave up, and quietly turned his vessel back to Spain and home. At last, however, the remaining three ships came out into the South Sea. It seemed so smooth and peaceful after the stormy Atlantic that Magellan called it *El Mar Pacifico,* the Pacific Ocean.

Now the men felt that they had done enough. They had found the way into the South Sea; they were running short of provisions; they had been voyaging for well over a year; they wanted to return home. It would have been the sensible course, at that; but Magellan had started out to find the Spice Islands, and that was what he intended to do.

Magellan's ships battled through the straits

"I'll go on and do my work if I have to eat the leather off the ship's yards," he said, and he meant it. He had no idea of the size of the Pacific, no suspicion that he was fated to sail for ninety-eight days, or over three months, without sight of land and with no chance to secure food or any fresh water except what could be caught in canvases when it rained.

It was a terrible voyage. Every crumb of food was eaten, even "the pouder that remayned thereof beinge now full of woorms," as Pigafetta wrote. The men caught rats in the holds and ate them, and then they did indeed strip the leather from the yards and trail it overboard to soften it before chewing it for what little nourishment it contained. The men had scurvy, and their teeth fell out and great sores spread over their bodies. Many died before, in March, 1521, they came upon the Ladrone Islands and then the Philippines, where they found plenty of food.

But here Magellan met his death. In a fight with the natives of the island of Mactan he was thrust through and through with spears. "Thus," wrote Pigafetta, "died our mirror, our comforter, our true guide; when they wounded him, he turned back many times to see whether we were all safe in the boats." In spite of what he had demanded of his crews, they had learned to love and respect this lame bulldog of a man.

The surviving sailors burned one ship, and another, the *Trinidad,* was so leaky she was not able to proceed. The remaining vessel, the *Victoria,* was loaded with spices and turned west toward Africa. Magellan had not really planned to sail around the earth, but it seemed to Juan Sebastián del Cano, now in charge, that it was easier to go forward around Africa's Cape of Good Hope than go backward across the awful wastes of the Pacific. He reached Spain after many difficulties on September 6, 1522, having completed a voyage that has been called the greatest feat of navigation ever performed before or since.

The expedition had been gone for three years, and of the five ships and 243 men who had set out, only one ship and eighteen gaunt and haggard sailors returned. But those eighteen could make a boast no one else would ever again be able to make: "*We were the first to circumnavigate the globe!*"

They were the first, also, to gain an idea of the true size of the earth.

7

The French

MAGELLAN'S voyage turned attention to the north. To avoid the hard route he had taken to the Spice Islands, another way into the Pacific must be found. He and others had shown that the long coastline between the Carolinas and the Strait of Magellan was unbroken. The only place left to look for a passageway was the north. The search for this passage occupied many men for well over three centuries, and when it was discovered by Sir Robert McClure about a hundred years ago it proved to be impractical. But the early explorers could not know that.

One of the searchers was Henry Hudson, an Englishman sailing for both his own country and the Dutch. Twice he tried to reach the Orient for England by crossing the North Pole, but was defeated by the ice. In 1609, under the Dutch flag, he was again turned back by ice and the mutiny of his crew. Now that his employer's plan had failed, he felt free to take matters into his own hands and try another route, farther south and west. In the

Half Moon he reached the mouth of the Hudson River and explored it as far as what is now Albany, New York. He did not discover the river; French and Portuguese seamen had been there before him. But his voyage established future land claims for the Dutch.

The next year Hudson was back working for England. This was typical of him. He was an undecided and colorless sort who could not seem to make up his mind or command the respect of his men. In just one way he was outstanding. His passion for discovery was so great that it led him into places that would have dismayed braver and better leaders. In the *Discovery* he entered Hudson Bay and spent over a year trying to find a way

Hudson's crew set him adrift

out to the west. When the crew, who had been frozen into th. ice pack for one winter and had barely survived, learned that Hudson's burning curiosity would not allow him to return sensibly home, they set him adrift in a small boat with his young son and a few loyal friends. He was never heard of again. One thing he accomplished: he proved the uselessness of trying to sail around America to the north, and so limited to other places the search for a westward passage.

France was by far the most active nation in this search. The French explorers were probably the best and greatest the world has ever known. They were as tough and hardy as the Spanish; but unlike the Spaniards they tried to understand and befriend the natives. They traded with them instead of enslaving them and seizing their wealth, which consisted of furs. Their conduct won them the liking and respect of the Canadian tribes, who helped them in many ways.

The first of these great Frenchmen was the bold, keen-featured Jacques Cartier, who sailed into the mouth of the St. Lawrence in 1535. Hudson's experience had taught Cartier that a sea passage straight through to the Pacific was unlikely; but he thought there might be a chain of rivers and lakes he could follow. Of course, he had no idea of the enormous distance involved. His three small vessels made their way up the river past the high bluff now occupied by Quebec, until they could go no further. Then the party took to little rowboats and pressed on between the walls of the forest, which was brilliant with autumn foliage and lively with flocks of ducks and geese and herds of moose and deer. Finally the Frenchmen came to Hochelaga, where Montreal now stands.

Hochelaga was the stronghold of the Huron-Iroquois Indians, as Tenochtitlán was of the Aztecs; but what a difference! Here, instead of a well-built, wealthy city, was a poor collection of bark and pole long houses, each sheltering several families. The whole encampment was surrounded by a rude palisade of tree trunks. The chief of these people, in contrast to Montezuma, was

a paralyzed and helpless old man, dressed in skins and wearing a red band embroidered with porcupine quills on his greasy black hair. But he made the visitors welcome in his way, showering them with gifts of corn, beans, and venison and inviting them to a feast.

Although the food set before them was unappetizing to the Frenchmen, they ate it politely and gave the Indians knives, hatchets, bright beads, and pewter rings. Thus was a friendship sealed. The Indians willingly guided the party upriver until they were halted by foaming rapids. Since Cartier was looking for China and this was what he had found, he named these the Lachine, or China, Rapids, as a sort of joke; and so they are

The chief made Cartier and his men welcome

known even today. It was too late in the season now to try to sail home to France across the stormy sea, so Cartier and his men wintered on their ships. They learned from the Indians to drink spruce tea to prevent scurvy: a piece of information valuable to later explorers. More valuable still was the reputation that Cartier made; as a result of it the Indians trusted and cooperated with future Frenchmen.

Cartier made a second voyage in 1541, then because of wars and internal troubles France did not send out another great explorer for sixty years. This was Samuel de Champlain, who became the founder of Canada. Champlain was a remarkable man. He was brave, energetic, unselfish, and deeply religious; and he had a scientific mind and imagination. In fact, he was the first to suggest the Panama Canal, although everyone thought he was insane at the time; and his journals give us the best descriptions we have of what America was like before the white men changed it.

By 1603, when Champlain started exploring the eastern part of Canada and the United States, it was generally accepted that these regions held no fabulous treasures of gold and gems. The wealth here was furs, fish, and lumber. To profit from these useful resources, some system for collecting them had to be set up. Among the many other things that he accomplished in his various trips to the New World, Champlain established fur trading posts all along the St. Lawrence; chief of them was Quebec. Here he built a village of strong wooden houses, surrounded

Champlain established fur trading posts

by vegetable gardens and enclosed by a palisade. The Iroquois no longer inhabited the St. Lawrence River valley, and by helping the local Hurons and Algonquins against this tribe, who were their bitter enemies, Champlain gained staunch allies. Soon Quebec was surrounded by a fringe of wigwams and long houses, and the French and the Hurons and Algonquins lived together as good neighbors.

Champlain was not a settler at heart, however, but an explorer. He sailed the long distance from Quebec to Hyannis on Cape Cod, investigating every one of the thousands of bays, inlets, and rivers of the New England coast and writing careful descriptions of the things he saw; cod and eels, minks and foxes, grapes and cranberries, and the look of the land. He was completely in love with the New World and wanted nothing better than to learn all he could about it.

When his Indian friends told him of a lake somewhere up the St. Lawrence, he turned his attention in that direction. He, like Cartier, was stopped by the Lachine Rapids; but, as he wrote, "It troubled me exceedingly to be obliged to return without having seen so great a lake, full of fair islands and bordered with the fine countries which they had described to me." Unlike Cartier, he went on in Indian canoes and turned south to discover lovely Lake Champlain. Later, with his Indian guides, he pushed on

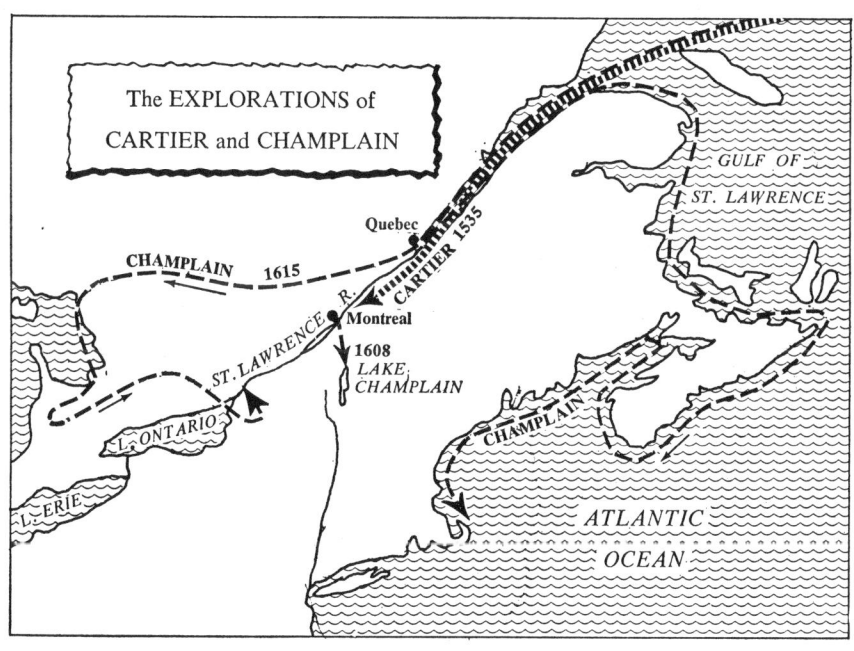

as far as Lake Ontario and Lake Huron, the furthest west any white man had been in this northern land which he claimed for France.

Another very valuable service he did for his country was to establish the custom of sending white youths to live among the Indians and learn their language and customs. These young men became known as *coureurs de bois,* or rangers of the woods. They were a class absolutely without equal in the exploration of America. They did not try to civilize the Indians, but rather became almost Indian themselves. They were wild and brave and restless, far more at home in the wilderness than in towns. Singly or in pairs, they roved far, safe in the confidence of their Indian brothers; and they brought back furs and valuable information to the French. Without them, knowledge of the continent would have been much slower in coming, and France would never have gained her stronghold in Canada.

Champlain died at Quebec on Christmas Day of 1635. One of his followers said of him, "His dauntless courage was matched by an unwearied patience . . . an earnest and generous nature, too ardent to criticize, too honorable to doubt the honor of others." A generation after his visit to the Hurons, the old chiefs remembered with astonishment the self-command, straightforwardness, and bravery of this great explorer.

Although Champlain was dead, the work he had begun lived on. His *coureurs de bois* ranged further and further west, discovering the other Great Lakes and bringing back reports from the Indians of a tremendous river deep in the land. These stories were so persistent that the Intendant, or Attorney General, of Canada decided they should be investigated. Perhaps here was the long-sought passage to Asia. For the exploring task he named two well-qualified men. One was Louis Joliet, a Quebec-born fur-trader who was experienced in wilderness living and knew the Great Lakes country well. The other was a Jesuit priest, Father Jacques Marquette, a gentle and devout man who had been for several years in charge of a mission at Michillimackinac, where the three largest Great Lakes meet. The Indians knew and loved him and could be counted on to help him and his partner.

These woods-wise explorers provided themselves with the simplest of outfits. They had two light birch-bark canoes, a supply of smoked meat and parched corn, and a rough map they had drawn from information obtained from the Indians. On May 17, 1673, they and five companions left Michillimackinac, following the north shore of Lake Michigan to the Fox River, which they ascended. At the headwaters they portaged, or carried their canoes, across to the Wisconsin River and floated down it to the Mississippi. This was the river of rumor, and their object was to find out whether it emptied into the Atlantic or Pacific Ocean.

Day after day they floated along past forests and prairies and high bluffs and low marshlands thick with wild rice. At night they landed and built fires over which they cooked buffalo meat, venison, fish, or wild fowl. In fair weather they slept under the stars; or if it rained, under their overturned canoes. On and on

Day after day the explorers and their guides paddled

they paddled, through country that the eyes of white men had never seen before. Although they met many Indians, they had no trouble with them. Their Indian friends at Michillimackinac had given them a calumet, or peace pipe, to show to these southern tribes, and this acted as a passport. In fact, the chief difficulty lay in getting away from these people, who would have liked to feast and entertain them for weeks on end.

As the journey went on, Father Marquette suspected this river to be the one discovered by the Spaniard de Soto. When the voyagers came to the mouth of the Arkansas River, and the Arkansas Indians told them that the Mississippi emptied into a great gulf ten days' journey to the south, he was sure of it. The

The Indians told the explorers where the river ended

hot July weather of the South bothered these men from cool Canada, and since their mission of finding out where the Mississippi led was accomplished, they decided to turn back. Paddling against the swift current was much harder than drifting down it had been, but at length they arrived at Lake Michigan and home.

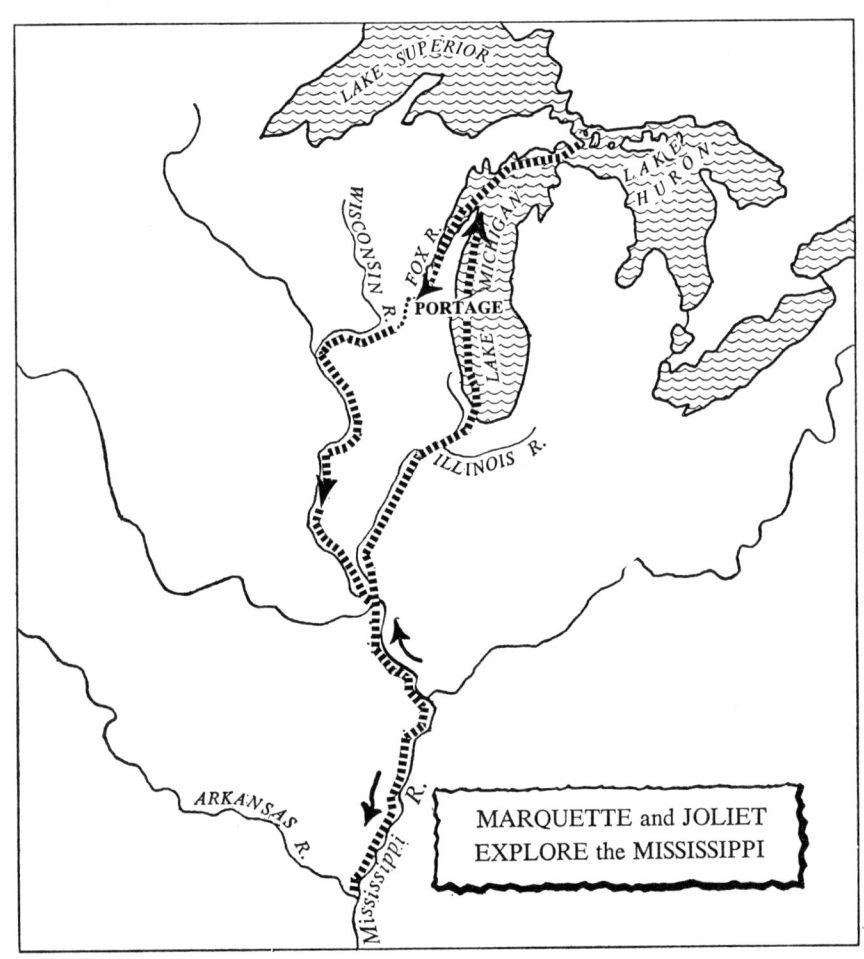

They had been gone four months, paddled two and a half thousand miles, and opened up the huge heart of the continent.

While all this was going on, the English colonies along the east coast were becoming strong and well established. If France was to keep control of the rich resources of the New World, she realized, she too should strengthen her position. Marquette and Joliet had established a claim for France, but that would not be enough. Forts and trading posts would have to be built to enforce the claim. Before this could be done, the land must be explored more thoroughly. To do this job, Robert Cavalier de La Salle was chosen.

La Salle has been called a man of iron because of his almost inhuman ability to endure hardship, and his stubborn determination to finish anything he started. He was tall, handsome, and well-educated, but almost everyone feared and disliked his harsh and overbearing manner—except the Indians. He had an odd knack for getting along with them.

He planned his exploration of the Mississippi well. In 1679 he built the first ship ever to sail the Great Lakes, *Le Griffon*. She took him, his men, and their supplies to Lake Michigan, where he erected a fort, sending *Le Griffon* back with a cargo of furs to buy more supplies. Then he pushed on by canoe to the banks of the St. Joseph and the Illinois rivers, where he built two more forts, one of which he named Fort Crève-Coeur—Fort Heartbreak. His idea was good: he planned to leave a chain of strongholds behind him for retreat in case of emergency.

But everything went wrong. *Le Griffon* disappeared, evidently sunk in winter storms. The men waited and waited for the desperately needed supplies at Fort Crève-Coeur—or Heartbreak, a good name for it. When these did not come, they grew mutinous. More than once they tried to kill La Salle, and desertion was common throughout the miserable winter.

As spring approached, La Salle knew he must go for help. With a few companions and an Indian guide he set out to walk through a thousand miles of wilderness to Montreal. It was the worst possible time of year to travel. The woods were hip-deep in spongy snow and the streams were swollen high above their banks. Game was scarce, and fires hard to light. Often, after crossing a river on a rude raft, the men had to sleep in wet clothes that froze before morning. By the time they reached Lake Erie, all five of La Salle's companions—trained woodsmen—were worn out.

But not La Salle. His iron will kept him on his feet. He alone ferried the sick men across to Fort Niagara, left them there, and with three fresh men went on to Montreal. There he collected supplies and returned to Fort Heartbreak on the Illinois. When he arrived he found the place burned flat by Indians and all his men gone.

Almost anybody else would have given up then and there; but La Salle's strength lay in not knowing when he was defeated. It took him two years to make new preparations, but finally he was able to set out to fulfill his long ambition: to travel the whole

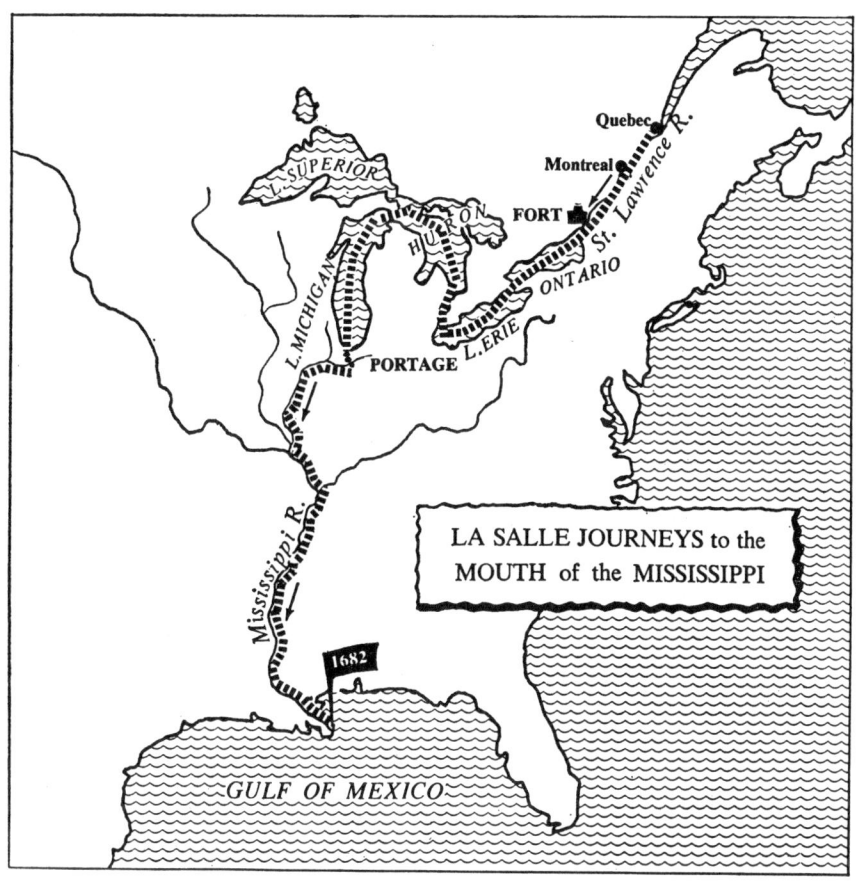

length of the Mississippi. He started the trip in December, 1681, and four months later came out on the lowlands of the delta and saw the Gulf of Mexico before him.

The banners of Heaven's King advance,
The mystery of the Cross shines forth,

sang the travel-weary adventurers as they planted a cross in the marshy soil and buried a leaden plate engraved with the arms of France. With this act they claimed for their king all the land drained by the great river they had been the first to explore fully; in his honor they named the territory Louisiana. In their wildest imaginings they could not have pictured what this claim meant. It included everything from the Canadian border to the Gulf of Mexico, and from the green ridges of the Alleghenies to the forbidding wall of the Rockies. It was the largest territory ever won for a monarch through the efforts of one of his subjects.

La Salle's end is sad. On a later trip by sea, the ship's captain lost his bearings and put La Salle and his followers ashore on the fever-ridden, marshy coast of Texas. For two years the abandoned men struggled against starvation, snakebite, illness, and the Indians. Then La Salle and the few survivors started out to work their way through thousands and thousands of wilderness miles to Montreal. The men finally mutinied against their leader; he was shot through the head, stripped of his clothes, spat upon, and left for wolves and buzzards to eat. When Henri de Tonti, commandant of Fort Crève-Coeur, heard of his death he formed an expedition to find his comrade's body, but with no success. With all his faults, La Salle was a brave man and deserved a better fate than murder in the wilderness. But at the last, one friend, de Tonti, stood staunch.

La Salle's death marks the end of the period of early exploration in the Americas. But the age of exploration will never cease

La Salle and his men struggled through the forest

as long as curious and courageous men dream of conquering the unknown. The list of great explorers is long, but it is by no means completed. In the future, other names—whose, we do not yet know—will be added to those of Columbus, Magellan, Champlain, and the others, as heroes of all time.

Other Books To Read

BAKELESS, KATHERINE *They Saw America First.* J. B. Lippincott Co., 1957

DUVOISIN, ROGER *And There Was America.* Alfred A. Knopf, 1938

HODGES, C. WALTER *Columbus Sails.* Coward-McCann, 1950

KJELGAARD, JAMES ARTHUR *Explorations of Père Marquette.* Random House, 1951

SHIPPEN, KATHERINE B. *Leif Eriksson.* Harper & Brothers, 1951

SPERRY, ARMSTRONG *The Voyages of Christopher Columbus.* Random House, 1950

SYME, RONALD *Cortés of Mexico.* William Morrow & Co., 1951

SYME, RONALD *La Salle of the Mississippi.* William Morrow & Co., 1953

SYME, RONALD *Magellan, First around the World.* William Morrow & Co., 1953

THARP, LOUISE HALL *Champlain, Northwest Voyager.* Little, Brown & Co., 1944

Acknowledgment

IN preparing this account of New World explorers, the author has found many books most helpful, among them the following especially: John Fiske, *The Discovery of America;* Leland Dewitt Baldwin, *The Story of the Americas;* Bernal Diaz Del Castillo, *The True History of the Conquest of Peru;* Richard Hakluyt, *Principall Navigations;* Sir Arthur Helps, *Spanish Conquests;* Francis Parkman, *The Struggle for a Continent;* Samuel de Champlain, *Journals;* William H. Prescott, *The Conquest of Peru, The Conquest of Mexico;* Snorre Sturlason, *Heimskringla, or the Lives of the Norse Kings;* G. M. Gathorne-Hardy, *The Norse Discoverers of America.*

Index

Africa, 21, 52, 53
Alabama, 43
Albany, New York, 55
Algonquin Indians, 10, 11, 60
Alleghenies, the, 70
America, 30, 56, 59
Americas, the 2, 29, 30, 47, 48, 70
Arctic, 30
Arkansas Indians, 65
Arkansas River, 65
Asia, 12, 19, 29, 48, 63
Atahualpa, 41, 42
Atlantic Ocean, 21, 24, 50, 63
Aztecs, the, 33, 35–38, 43, 57

Bahamas, the, 27
Balboa, Vasco Nuñez de, 32–34, 49
Bermejo, Juan Rodriguez, 27
Brazil, 30, 49

Cabot, John, 29
Cabral, Pedro Alvares, 30
Canada, 56, 59, 62, 63, 66, 70
Canary Islands, the, 24

Cano, Juan Sebastián del, 53
Cape Cod, 60
Cape of Good Hope, 53
Carolinas, the, 30, 43, 54
Cartier, Jacques, 56–59, 61
Champlain, Lake, 61
Champlain, Samuel de, 59–62, 72
Charles V, King (Spain), 49
Chickasaws, the, 43
China, 57
Christianity, 41
Cipangu (*see* Japan)
Columbus, Christopher, 12, 20–30, 32, 49, 72
Conquistadors, 31–47
Constantinople, 19
Coronado, Francisco, 44–47
Cortés, Hernán, 33, 35–38, 41
Coureurs de bois, 62
Crève-Coeur, Fort, 67, 68, 70
Cuba, 33
Cuzco, 41

de Soto, Hernando, 43, 44, 65

Discovery, the, 55
Dutch, the, 54, 55

earth—
   shape of, 12–14
   size of, 53
East, the, 19, 48, 54
East Indies, the, 21
England, 29, 54, 55, 67
Eric the Red, 4, 8, 9
Erie, Lake, 68
Europe, 12, 15, 19, 39, 47
Everest, Mount, 2

Faroes, the, 15
Florida, 31, 32, 43
Fountain of Youth, the, 32
Fox River, 63
France, 30, 54–72
fur trading, 59–62

Genoa, 20
German maps, 30
gold, 30–44
Grand Canyon, 44, 45
Great Lakes, the, 62, 63, 67
Great Plains, the, 44, 46
Greenland, 4, 7–10, 15
Griffon, le, 67, 68
Guayaquil, Gulf of, 39

Half Moon, the, 55
Harald Fairhair, King, 9
Heartbreak (*see* Crève-Coeur, Fort)
Helluland, 8
Herjulf, 4
Herjulfson, Bjarni, 4–8

Hillary, Sir Edmund, 2
Hochelaga, 57
Hudson Bay, 55
Hudson, Henry, 54–56
Hudson River, 55
Huron-Iroquois Indians, 57
Huron, Lake, 62
Hurons, the, 60, 62
Hyannis, 60

Iceland, 7–10, 15
Illinois River, 67, 68
Inca, 39, 41–43
India, 49
Indies, the, 38
Iroquois, the, 60
Isabella, Queen, 23, 27
Italy, 19

Japan, 23, 27
Joliet, Louis, 63, 66, 67

Kansas, 44
knorr, 4, 5

Labrador, 8
Lachine (China) Rapids, 57, 61
Ladrone Islands, 52
La Salle, Robert Cavalier de, 67–71
latitude, 16
Leif (son of Eric the Red), 8
Leoncico, 33
longitude, 17
Louisiana, 70

Mactan, 52
Magellan, Ferdinand, 48–54, 72

76

Magellan, Strait of, 50, 54
Malay, 49
Manuel, King, 49
Mar del Sur, el (*see* South Sea)
Mare Tenebrosum (*see* Sea of Darkness)
Mar Pacifico, el (*see* Pacific Ocean)
Markland, 8, 12
Marquette, Father Jacques, 63, 65–67
Massachusetts, 9
McClure, Sir Robert, 54
Mexico, 33, 35, 42, 44, 46
Mexico City, 35
Mexico, Gulf of, 69, 70
Michigan, Lake, 63, 66, 67
Michillimackinac, 63, 65
Mississippi, 43
Mississippi River, 43, 63, 65–67, 69
Montezuma, 35–38, 41, 57
Montreal, 57, 68, 70
Morocco, 49
Mundus Novus (*see* New World, the)
Muskogee Indians, 43
mutiny, 26, 27, 49, 50, 54–56, 70

navigation, 7, 16–18, 23–28, 49–53, 54–70
Nebraska, 44
New England, 8, 9, 60
Newfoundland, 8
New World, the, 3, 9, 10, 27, 29–31, 47–49, 59, 61, 67
Niagara, Fort, 68
Niña, the, 23, 24
Noche Triste, la (Sorrowful Night), 38
Norgay, Tenzing, 2

North America, 8–10, 27, **30**
North Atlantic, 4, 15
North Pole, 54
Norway, 4, 7, 9, 10
Nova Scotia, 8, 30

Ontario, Lake, 62
Orient (*see* East, the)
Ottoman Turks (*see* Turks, the)

Pacific Ocean, 50, 52–54, 56, 63
Palos, 23
Panama, 32
Panama Canal, 59
Panama, Isthmus of, 33
Pascua Florida, 32
Peru, 39, 41, 43
Philippines, the, 52
Pigafetta, Antonio, 49, 52
Pinta, the, 23, 24
Pizarro, Francisco, 38–43
Ponce de León, 31, 32
Porto Santo, 20–22
Portugal, 20, 30, 49, 55
Puerto Rico, 32

Quebec, 56, 59, 60, 62, 63
Quetzalcoatl, 35
Quito, 41

Rockies, the, 70

"sailors' vapors," 16
St. Joseph River, 67
St. Lawrence River, 56, 59–61
Santa Maria, the, 23
Santo Domingo, 32

Sargasso Sea, the, 14, 24
scurvy, 15, 52, 59
Sea of Darkness, 13, 21
Shetlands, the, 15
ships—
   conditions on, 16, 25, 26, 49–53
   construction of, 4, 5, 16
shipworms, 15
South America, 32, 38, 49, 50
South Sea, 33, 50
Spain, 23, 25, 29–47, 49, 50, 53, 56, 65
Spaniards (*see* Spain)
Spice Islands, the, 48–50, 54
spice trade, the, 19, 21, 48

Temple of the Sun, the, 39
Tennessee, 43
Tenochtitlán, 35, 36, 57
Texas, 70
Tonti, Henri de, 70

treasure (*see* gold)
Trinidad, the, 52
Tumbes, 39
Turks, the, 19

United States, 59
United States Southwest, 43

Vera Cruz, 35
Verrazano, Giovanni da, 30
Vespucci, Amerigo, 29, 30
Victoria, the, 52
Vikings, the, 4–10, 12, 15, 27, 29
Vinland, 9, 12

Western Hemisphere, the, 12, 47
Wineland, 9
Wisconsin River, 63
Woodland, 8

Zuñi Indians, 44

About the Author

Louise Dickinson Rich has always been interested in the early history of America. Growing up in Plymouth Country, Massachusetts, she knew the coast explored by the Vikings and heard many tales of the early exploration of New England. She has lived in Vermont and on the coast of Maine, in country known to Samuel de Champlain and others of the early explorers. To her, they have always seemed men who are very much alive. As she did research work on her previous book, THE FIRST BOOK OF THE EARLY SETTLERS, the many references to the explorers who had preceded the settlers aroused her interest further, and she decided to write THE FIRST BOOK OF NEW WORLD EXPLORERS.

She still lives in Massachusetts, and spends summers on the coast of Maine, near Mount Desert Island, which was visited and named by Champlain. New England has been the background for her many books, among them *We Took to the Woods, The Peninsula, The Start of the Trail,* and *The First Book of New England.*

```
J          4-6          Copy I
973.1
R        Rich
           First book of New World
         explorers
```

Date Due

DISCARDED FROM THE
PORTVILLE FREE LIBRARY

PORTVILLE FREE LIBRARY
PORTVILLE, N. Y.

Member Of
Chautauqua-Cattaraugus Library System

 PRINTED IN U.S.A.